AN EARLY LEARNING FINANCIAL LITERACY PROGRAM

The Financial Literacy Guy's ABC Book

BY ANDREW SCOTT
ILLUSTRATED BY ALIVIA SCOTT

A

A
IS FOR
ASSET

B

B
IS FOR
BUDGET

C

C
IS FOR
CREDIT

D

D
IS FOR
DEBIT
CARD

E

E

IS FOR

ENTREPRENEUR

F

F
IS FOR
FICA
(FEDERAL INSURANCE CONTRIBUTION ACT)

G
IS FOR
GROSS INCOME

H

H
IS FOR
HOME EQUITY

I
IS FOR
INTEREST

J

J
IS FOR
JOB

K

K
IS FOR
KNOW YOUR
CUSTOMER

L

L
IS FOR
LOAN

M

M
IS FOR
MONEY

N

N
IS FOR
NET
INCOME

O
IS FOR
OVERDRAFT PROTECTION

P

P
IS FOR
PROFIT

Q

Q
IS FOR
QUALIFIED RETIREMENT ACCOUNT

R

R

IS FOR

RETURN ON INVESTMENT

(R.O.I)

S

S
IS FOR
SAVINGS

T

T
IS FOR
TAXES

U

U

IS FOR

UNIFORMED TRANSFER TO MINORS ACCOUNT

(UTMA)

V

V
IS FOR
VARIABLE

W

W
IS FOR
WEALTH

X

X

IS FOR

XD

Y

Y
IS FOR
YIELD

Z

Z
IS FOR
ZERO PERCENT INTEREST

Made in the USA
Middletown, DE
22 July 2025

11095634R00031